W9-AVD-291

THE FIRE DEPARTMENT

David and Patricia Armentrout

Rourke
Publishing LLC
Vero Beach, Florida 32964

© 2009 Rourke Publishing LLC

www.rourkepublishing.com

PHOTO CREDITS: © Francis Twitty: cover; © Melissa Carroll: page 5; © Frances Twitty: page 6; © Yvonne Chamberlain: page 8; © Rick Rhay: page 9; © Jim Parkin: page 10; © Paolo Florendo: page 11; © Tomaz Levstek: page 15; © Roberta Osborne: page 17; © Rarpia: page 18; © Blaney Photo: page 19; © Sean Locke: page 20; © Talk Kienas: page 21; © Milan Radulovic: page 22

Edited by Kelli Hicks

Cover design by Teri Intzegian
Interior design by Teri Intzegian

Library of Congress Cataloging-in-Publication Data

Armentrout, David, 1962-
  The fire department / David and Patricia Armentrout.
    p. cm. -- (Our community)
  ISBN 978-1-60472-336-6
  1. Fire stations--Juvenile literature. I. Armentrout, Patricia, 1960- II. Title.
  TH9148.A76 2008
  628.9'2--dc22
                                2008016348

Printed in the USA

CG/CG

Rourke Publishing

www.rourkepublishing.com – rourke@rourkepublishing.com
Post Office Box 3328, Vero Beach, FL 32964

Table of Contents

Fire Department

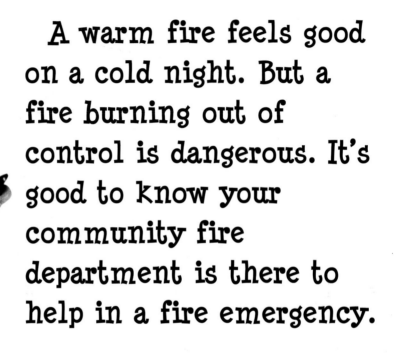

A warm fire feels good on a cold night. But a fire burning out of control is dangerous. It's good to know your community fire department is there to help in a fire emergency.

Firefighters work hard to keep communities safe.

What does a Firefighter Do?

Firefighters fight fire, but they also work to **prevent** them. Firefighters save lives and property.

Fire can spread quickly and destroy property.

A fire rescue team arrives
at an accident scene.

Training

Firefighting is a dangerous job. That's why firefighters spend a lot of time training. They learn how to put out fires and how to rescue people in danger.

Firefighters practice using safety **harnesses.**

A fire crew trains with air tanks.

The Fire Station

Firefighters work long shifts. While on duty, they work, eat, and sleep at the fire station. When an emergency call comes in, firefighters are ready to go.

Firefighters keep their trucks in good working order.

A firefighters tough equipment and fire
gear weighs about 60 pounds (27 kg).

Fighting Fire

Most people avoid danger, but firefighters search for it!

Firefighters know, where there is smoke, there is fire.

Firefighters rush to the scene of an emergency.

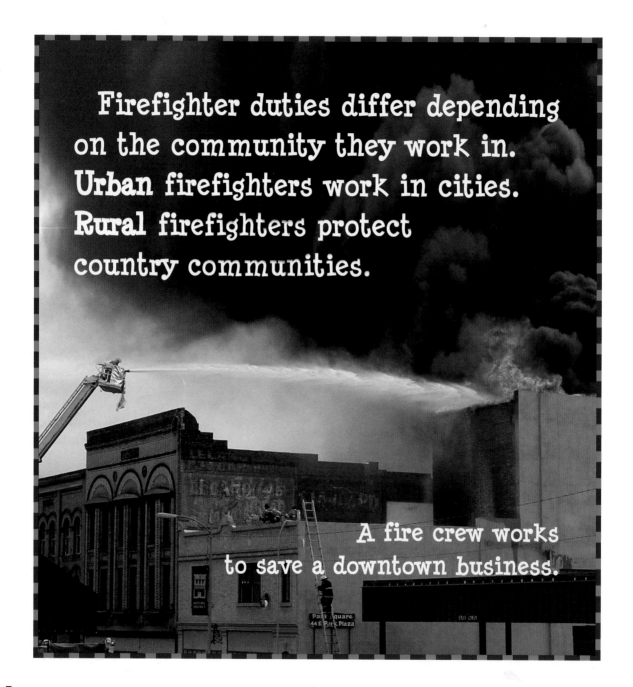

Firefighter duties differ depending on the community they work in. **Urban** firefighters work in cities. **Rural** firefighters protect country communities.

A fire crew works to save a downtown business.

Firefighters battle a wildfire.

Fire Trucks

Fire trucks are coming! Loud sirens and flashing lights warn everyone to get out of the way.

Fire trucks can cost over one million dollars each!

Tank trucks haul water to fires.
Pump trucks carry hoses and
pump water.

Ladder trucks haul ladders to fires. Firefighters use them to reach people trapped in tall buildings. The tallest ladders reach more than 100 feet.

Thick smoke rises from a burning building.

Prevention and Safety

Firefighters would rather prevent a fire than put one out. Firefighters teach children and other groups in their community about fire safety.

Kids learn how
fire equipment is used.

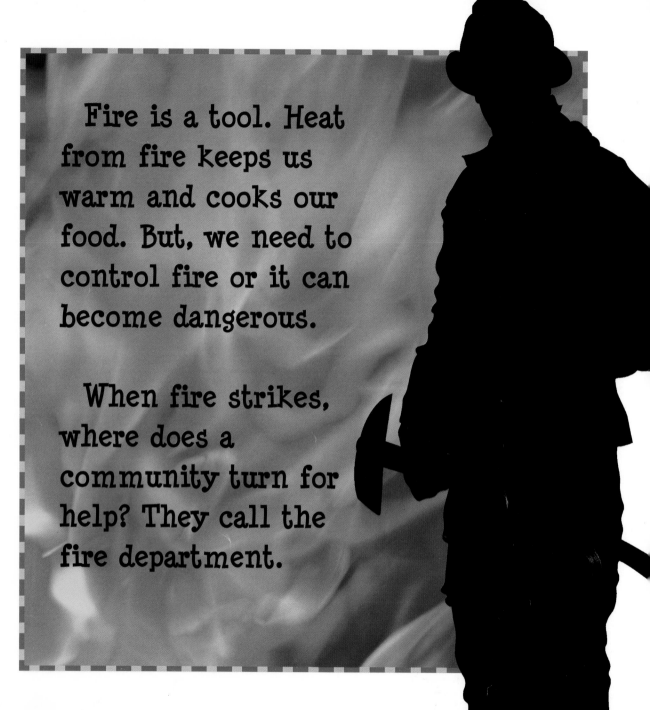

Fire is a tool. Heat from fire keeps us warm and cooks our food. But, we need to control fire or it can become dangerous.

When fire strikes, where does a community turn for help? They call the fire department.

Glossary

harnesses (HAR-niss-ez): straps used to keep people safe

prevent (pri-VENT): to stop something before it starts

rural (RUR-uhl): country or farming community

urban (UR-buhn): city community

INDEX

FURTHER READING

Raatma, Lucia. *Fire Safety.* Child's World, 2003.

Somervill, Barbara A. *First Response: By Air.* Children's Press, 2007.

Wheeler, Jill C. *Firefighters.* Checkerboard Books, 2002.

WEBSITES

www.firesafety.gov/kids/flash.shtm
www.firesafetyforkids.org
www.mcgruff.org

ABOUT THE AUTHORS

David and Patricia Armentrout specialize in nonfiction childrens books. They enjoy exploring different topics and have written about many subjects, including sports, animals, history, and people. David and Patricia love to spend their free time outdoors with their two boys and dog Max.